Warped Passage

poems and paintings

Acknowledgements

Many thanks to the editors of the magazines in which some of these pieces first appeared:
Second Sight in Beltway Poetry Journal*, Second Sight* (art*)* in Red Fez*, Portrait with Cracked Paint, Imaginary Conversation, Memory* (art and poems) in Mixitini Matrix, *Closing Mother Down* in Public Republic, *Closing Mother Down* (art) in Red Fez*, Fade* in Blood Orange Review, *Voyager* in VerseWrights, *Mother Forgets Church* in PANK*, Ninety* in THIS Literary Journal, *Ninety*(art) in Red Fez, *Wife* (art) in Red Fez.

We'd especially like to thank Cheryl A. Townsend for her photographs of the art in this collection.

for our mother

Warped Passage

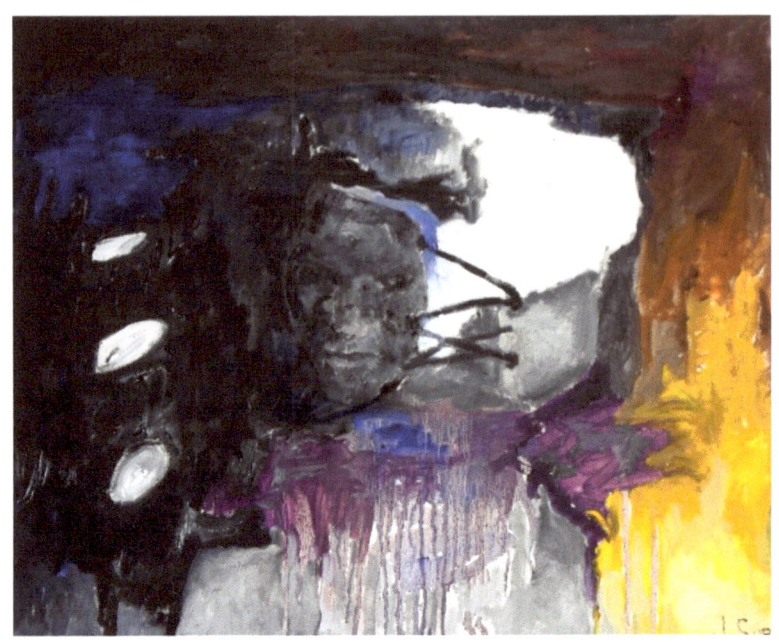

Sleight of Hand

The mouse. The improbable hole
breathing in the shape of the body.

At the lip of every tunnel an urge to escape
registers. The baseboard fills and empties
like a slippery memory.

Outside a woman thrashes a broom against
what she can't understand. Her mind is going dark—
but if a camel can pass through a needle's eye
shouldn't the brain believe almost anything?

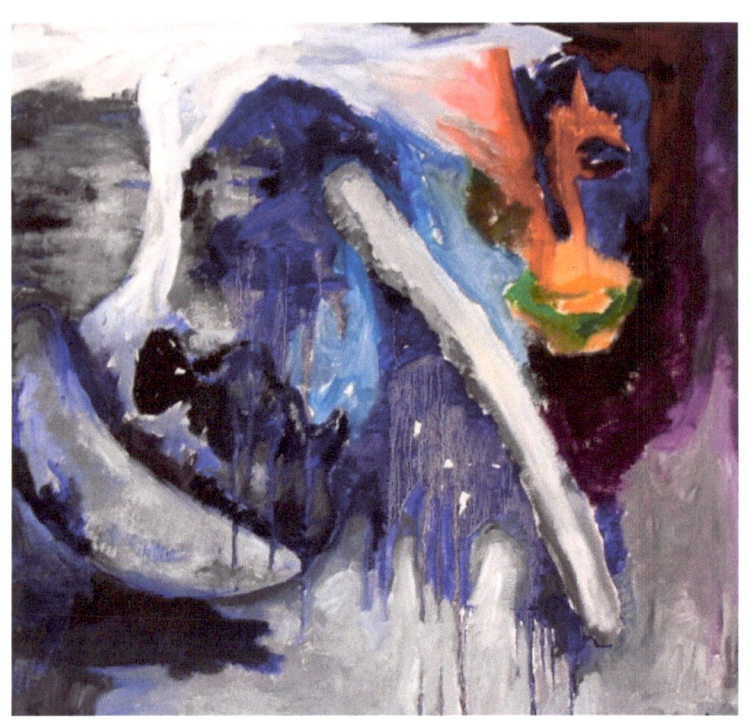

Second Sight

Along gallery corridors
the murmuring never stops.
Ginevra against the junipers,
her hair still alive. Her sullen mouth
is saying something about resurrection
something we cannot hear.

We are cordoned off by velvet ropes
and centuries of loss while she,
irises turned inward, can no longer see
the damage that distance does.

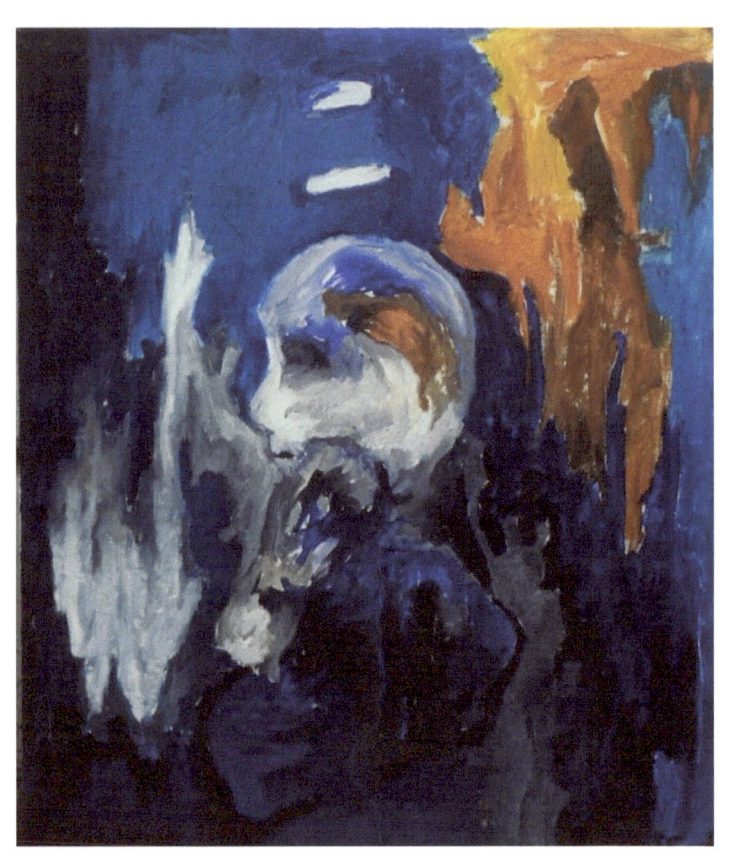

Portrait with Cracked Paint

Where canvas slackens
and stretches here
are the ears and eyes.

Cheekbones gleam
out of craquelure skin
and her head is a glazed bowl.
Something is
tipping her memory out.

There are tangles riveling
in her brain
shrinking it, blistering the colors
peeling the layers away.

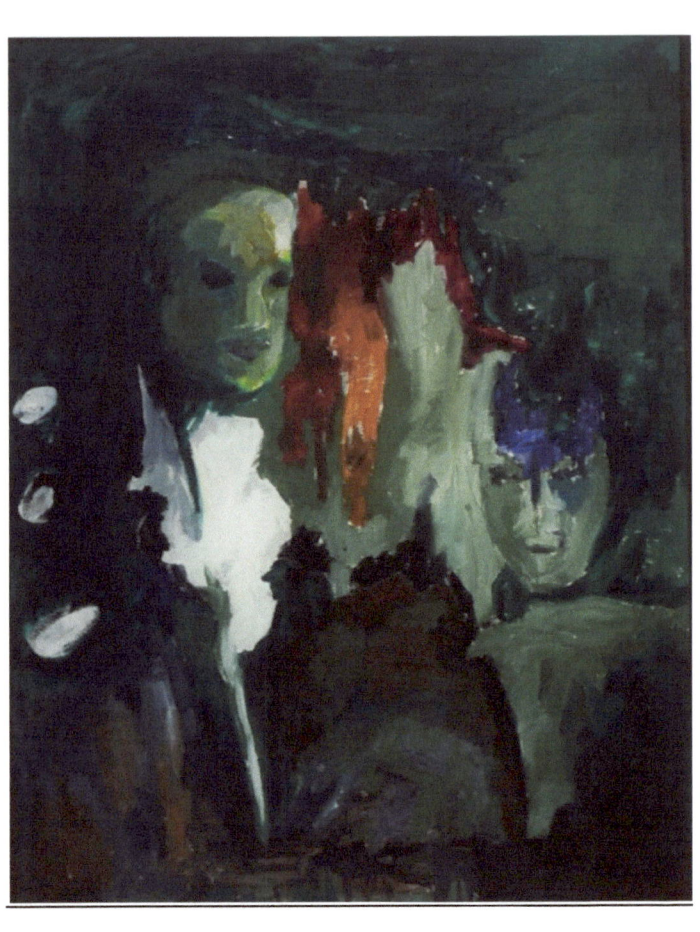

Voyager

She enters a room
as if it's an undiscovered island.
Where is my other house? I want to go home.
For her loss, I grieve. I cannot bear
to watch her wander, lost
in her small places. I remember how
she loved the panoramic—
the prairie she was born to,
the lake rocking our boat,
the cathedral ceilings in the living
room. Space made her feel safe.
Now she tells me she doesn't know
how to leave it; even as she steps
her small feet into my brother's big shoes
and slides them forward as a child might,
each one a boat to glide away in.

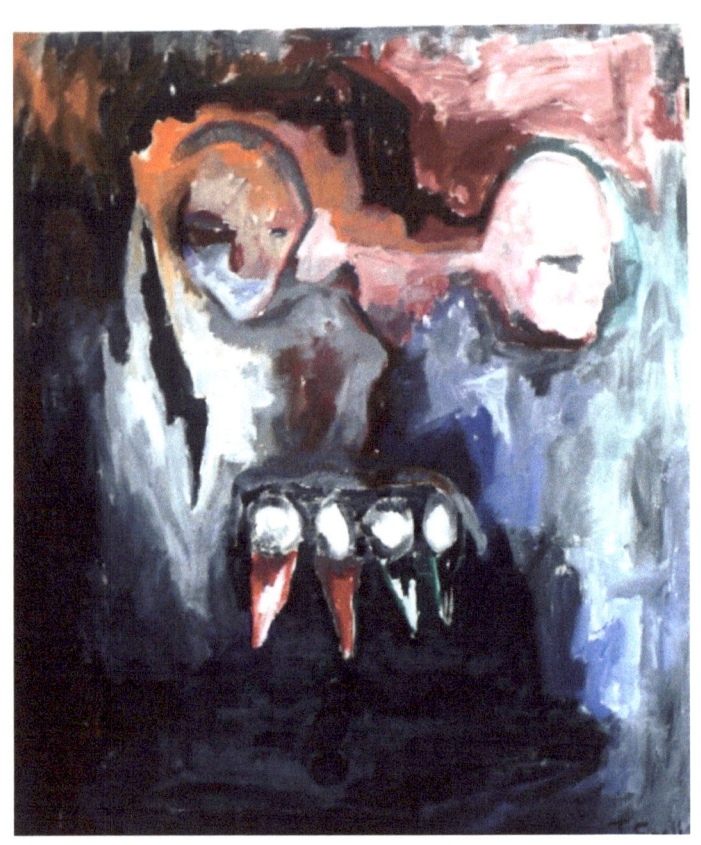

Closing Mother Down

I'm trimming my sister's hair
when Mother makes for the scissors.
I'm the one... she protests. Her words
sputter to a halt as I close the blades.

She's dwarfed in the kitchen
she once ruled and I picture her as she was
bending low over the children's curls
her movements precise and quick.

I am the edge cutting her from her past
and I know the quirks of scissors:
arms easily parted, but better together
though crossed as swords.

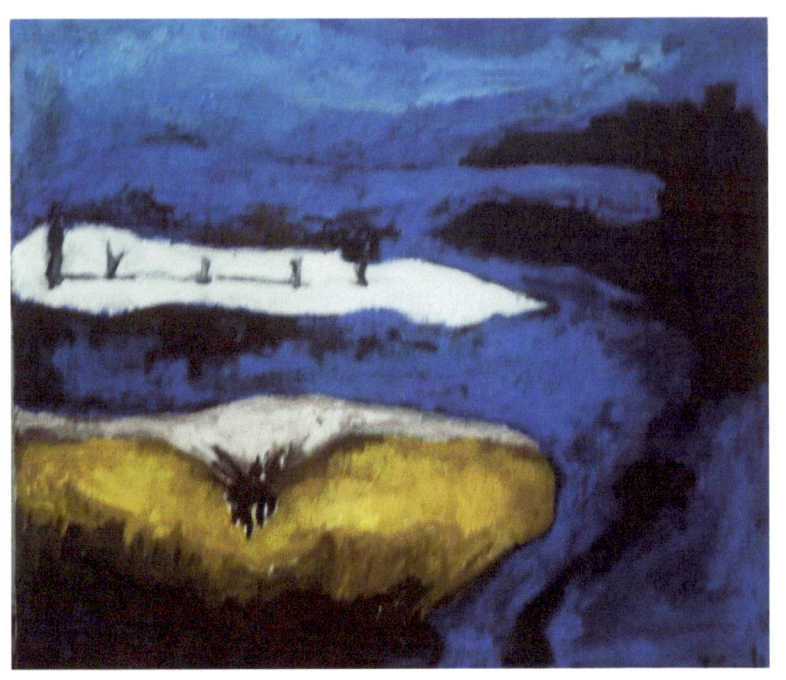

Fade

Afternoon sun smoothes
her quilted skin, her cheeks
rise under her eyes.

She's silent in the car
squints at streetlights flaring
up along the road.

She says nothing when I feed her,
but I see how she tracks the glint
bouncing off the spoon.

When downtown smog smudges
 her bedroom windowpane, I begin
to draw the drapes. She tugs at my wrist.

It's not enough, she says, *but let it in.*

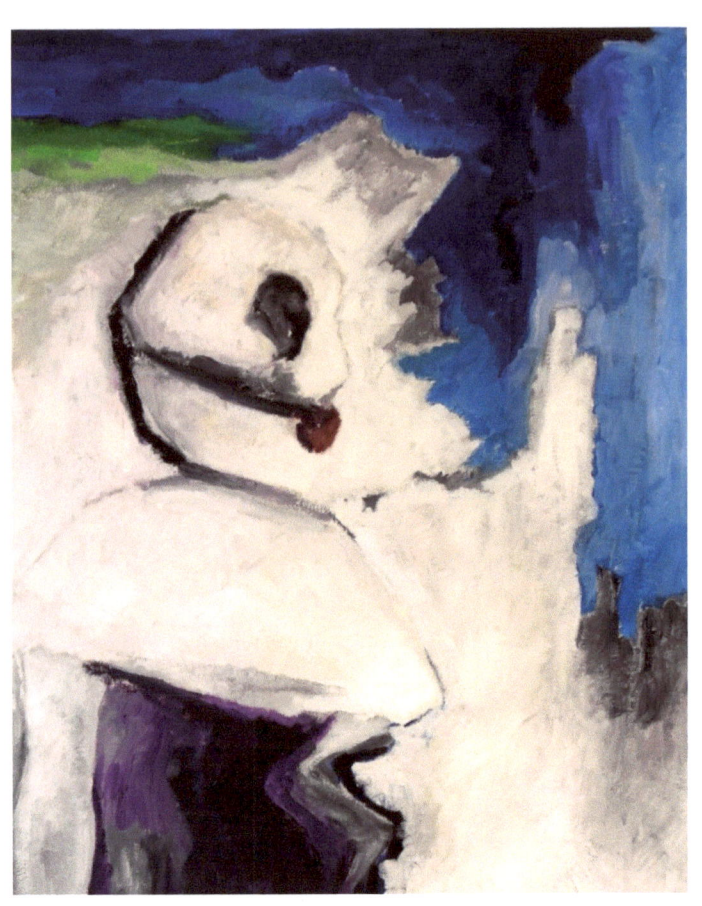

Mother Forgets Church

and a hush smothers us.
in her brain's atrium
a processional of tangles
son brother husband father.
Where's the church and where's the steeple?
she wanders empty-eyed
from the basilica   to the transept of the cross
all dressed up since 2 AM.

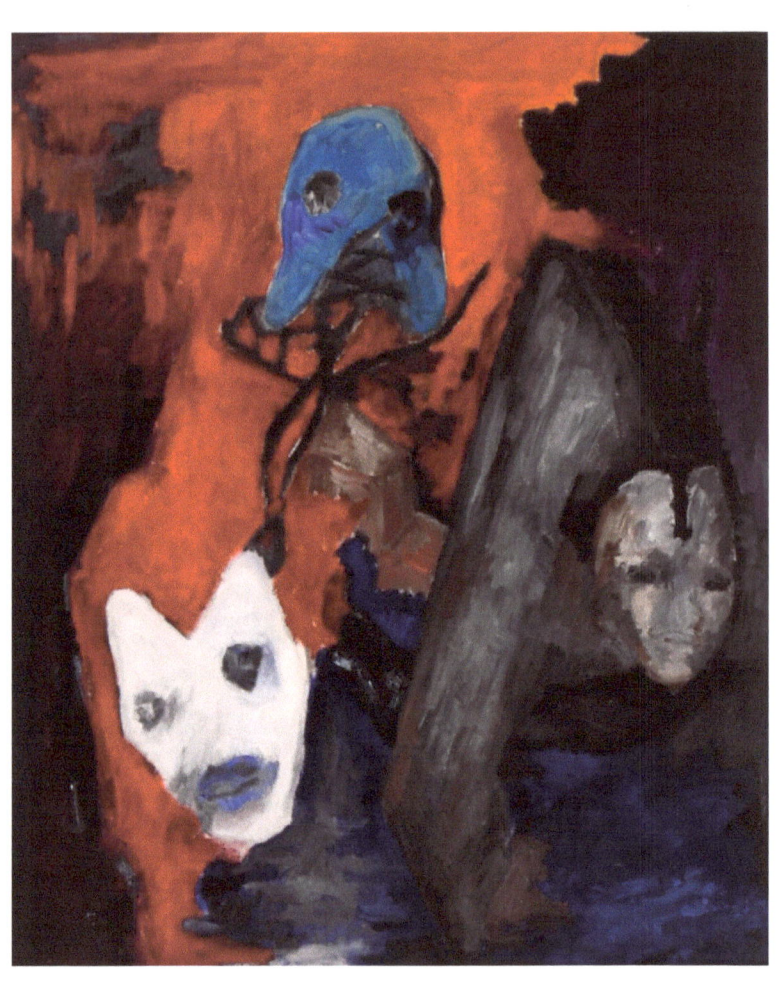

Lost

Along straggling streets
that will never connect them
the woman moves on. Her son
elbows through the crush
searching for any door left ajar
any wedge of light spilling
into the hooded evening.

He pulls keys out of his pocket
and tries every lock, but it's not easy
to find the way back home
when night curves without warning
the stars do not touch
the road stretches down to the sea.

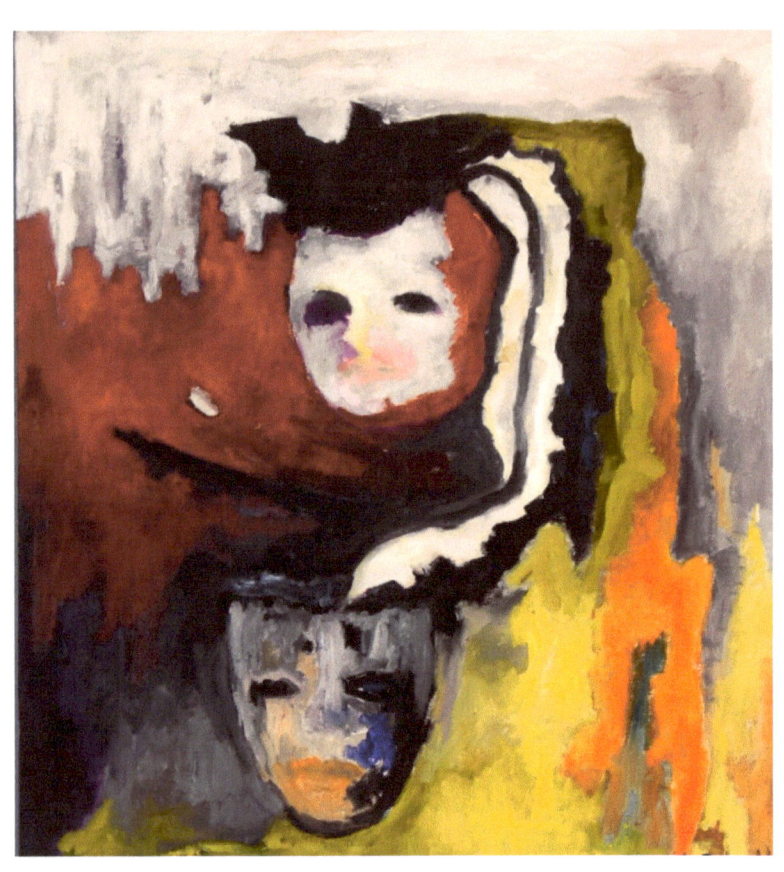

Memory

She cracks an egg over a skillet
and a bird flies up. Its feathers are dark
as the keys in the sugar bowl
the wallet in the freezer
the tangles in her brain.
What will take her out of the night
and into the blind spot
she mistakes for the sun?
May it gleam the sweet of her smile.
May it flicker its light upon her spine.
May it open wings-wide and beat for her
relentlessly as blood.

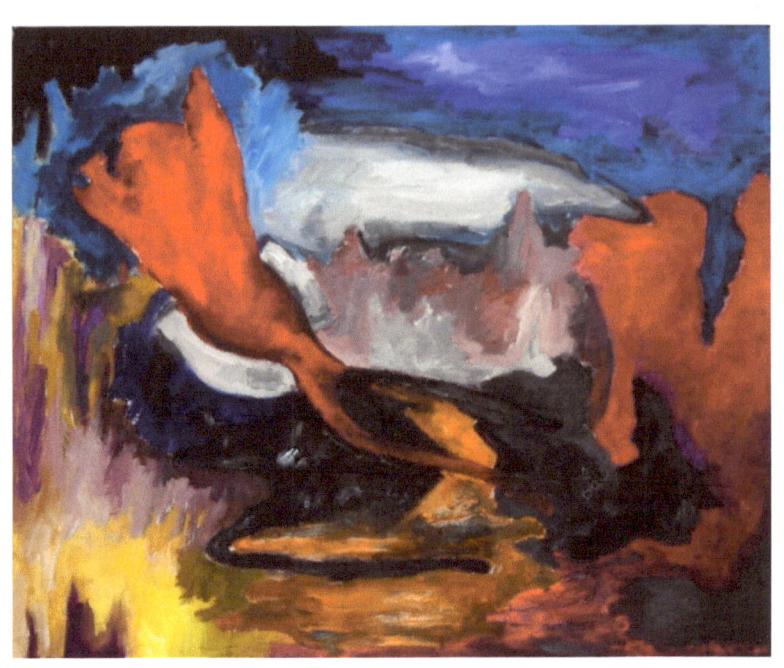

Poem Made of Sleep

Mother slips into sleep
beside the banked fire.
The red pulse at its core
warms her bones
but it's flesh
that keeps her rooted here
a steeple of fingers
under the chin.

When she opens scribbled lids
to dreams already pulling away
her hands, twined at the thumb
flutter. Along the route of her dark
migration, two birds follow one another
into the guttering shadows.

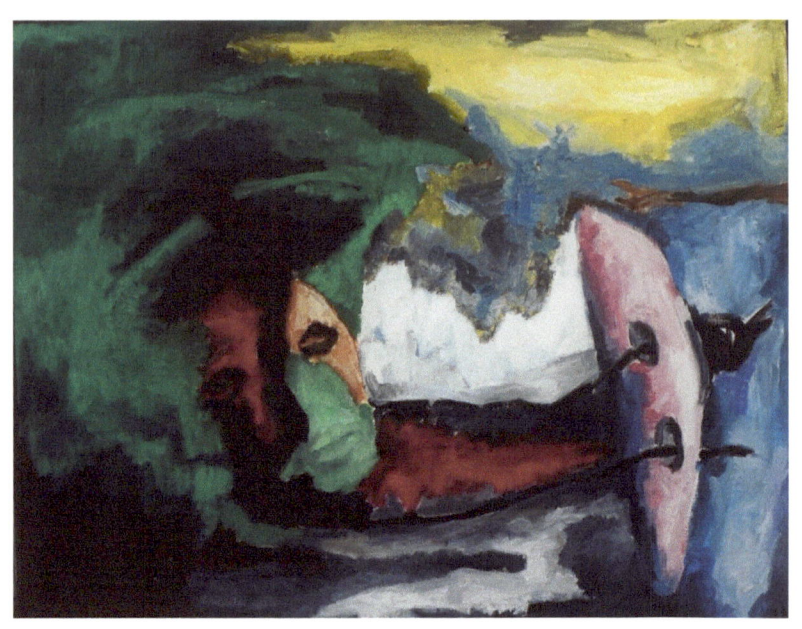

Ninety

I'm taking everything off
she announces, clawing at her clothes.
A new scar gleams on her mended hip.
Where did this come from, where is it going?

A cross-hatched seam
in the center of a body's landslide.
A cradle for children, a long-ago man;
a broken wing.

She begins brailing her fingertip down
the red raised tracks. It's not what she expected.
A railroad crossing pocked with stop signs.
A fire escape going down.

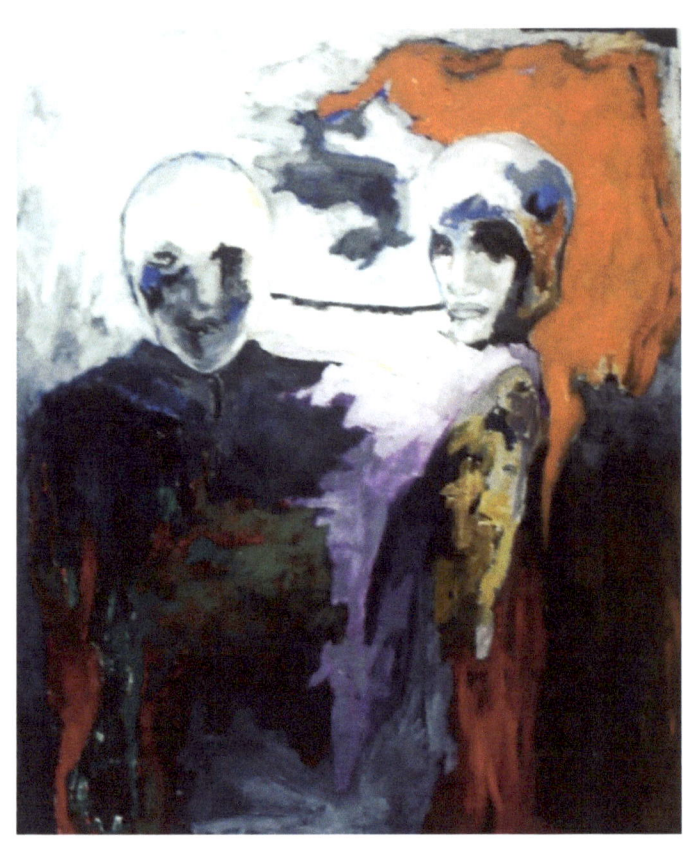

Pact

We never wanted the other
to suffer, though it was always
for someone's own good.
You locked me in. I shut you out.
You shook me by the shoulders.
I shook you to the core. So.
When you're dangling by a thread
I'll cut it for you. I'll do for you
what you did for me on the days
you pulled my milk-teeth out
dragging each one on its pulpy string
through a lifetime of slamming doors.

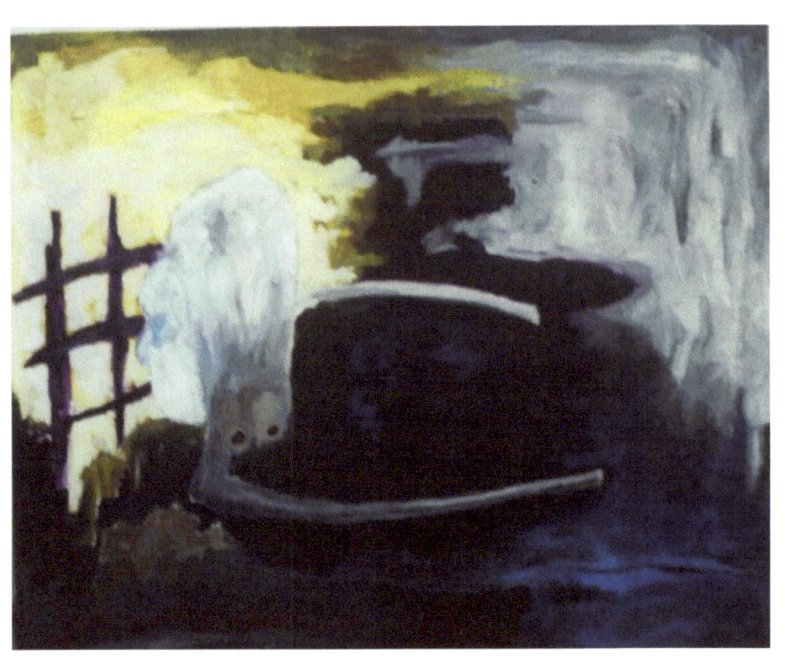

L'Heure Bleue

There's no climbing out
of blue this deep. I run my palms
along edges of the headboard
as if a boundary can prove the past
is not present here.

Across the hall, a light switches on
in my mother's bedroom. Notes
from her radio collide with lyrics
that travel much more slowly now.

The words insist we are fine
as we are but when the voice breaks off
between spikes of static, it reaches
toward me, sticky as fingers.

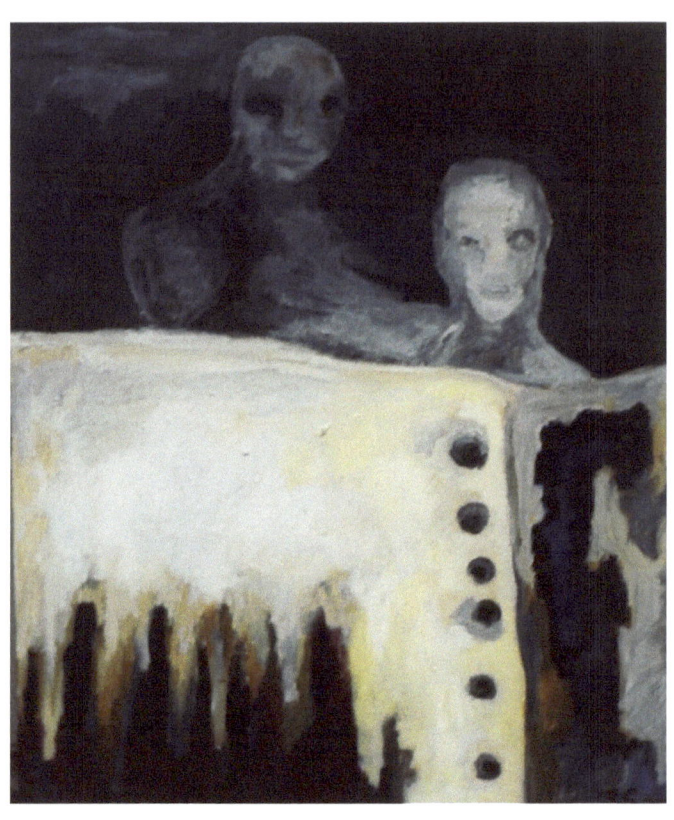

Wife

After her memory went
what was left was
her past
stacked in albums where
she looked at her life
as if lived by others
every page more faded—
but even as her children fell away
she brought the photos closer
to touch the only face not forgotten.
Oh, darling, she said, stroking his grainy cheek.

.

Cheryl Snell is the author of *Prisoner's Dilemma* and five other collections of poetry, and her most recent novel is *Shiva's Arms (Writer's Lair Books)*. Her poetry has appeared in many online and print journals, lately in The Curator, Olentangy Review, PANK, Deep Water Literary Journal, and Mixitini Matrix. She has had work chosen for a Best of the Net Anthology and other anthologies. **Janet Snell** is a magna cum laude graduate of the Maryland Institute, College of Art, where she studied painting with the late Edward Dugmore. She has been included in many group and solo shows, including New York's Drawing Center, Washington's Strathmore Hall, Cleveland's Spaces, and Akron's Summit Art Space. The author of FLYTRAP (Cleveland Poetry Center 1990) and an E-chapbook, HEADS (March Street Press 1998), one of her collections with Cheryl Snell, PRISONER'S DILEMMA, won the Lopside Press Chapbook Contest. Snell paints semi-realistic portraits on commission.